ZIGREX- POWER COACHING

THE RESURRECTION SERIES

TANYA KARUMBAIAH

Clever Fox® PUBLISHING
Chennai • Bangalore

CLEVER FOX PUBLISHING
Chennai, India

Published by CLEVER FOX PUBLISHING 2025

ISBN: 978-93-6707-034-5

Dedicated to those who refused to remain buried

To the souls who broke, rebuilt, and rose taller.

To the overlooked, the underestimated, the unheard—

until their presence became impossible to ignore.

This is not mere motivation.

This is reclamation.

This is your ascension.

CONTENTS

Acknowledgment .... *vii*

Introduction: From Ritual to Real — My Power Coaching Journey .... *ix*

Zigrex Power Coaching: The Resurrection Series .... *xi*

Before You Begin: Why This Book Exists .... *xiii*

1. The Collapse Before the Rise 3
2. Identity Resurrection: The Rise of the Inner Titan 8
3. Emotional Command: From Fragmented to Fearless 14
4. The Zigrex Will: Rituals for Ruthless Focus 21
5. Strategic Solitude: Silence as a Weapon 27
6. Financial Power: Energy, Strategy, Execution 35
7. The Public Self: Stage Presence, Visibility & Aura 43
8. Divine Detachment: The Exit from Neediness 50
9. The Inner Empire: Designing a Life of Sovereignty 57
10. Power Finale: The Zigrex Declaration 65

Author's Note *69*

ACKNOWLEDGMENT

My deepest gratitude to those who stood by me when I had nothing left but will.

To my parents—for instilling strength through discipline and dignity through resilience.

To Poonacha—for being both a mirror and a mystery, grounding me through turbulence.

And to the ones who doubted me—your silence became my sharpened blade.

This book is born not from peace, but from pressure.

Not from applause, but from persistence.

Thank you for shaping the fire I now carry forward.

INTRODUCTION: FROM RITUAL TO REAL — MY POWER COACHING JOURNEY

The Zigrex Codex was written in a ritualistic format — immersive, symbolic, and rooted in spiritual neuroscience. It was my way of encoding personal power through mystery, energy, and invocation. That format may have felt unfamiliar or unusual to some. And that's okay. It was one expression of power.

This Power Coaching Series, on the other hand, is written in a language more grounded, more direct — what you might call everyday power. It's still neuroscience. It's still deep, energetic work. But this time, it's framed in a way that anyone — especially those in survival mode — can understand and apply.

This is not a sanitized, polished version of me giving advice from a pedestal. Before every coaching session in this series, I've done a bit of my own shadow work — writing honestly about what I've been through. You'll see fragments of my own story, laid bare. Not for drama. Not for sympathy. But because this is a part of my healing journey too. This is how I integrate pain and power.

My life hasn't been easy. Some people are handed things. Others, like me, have to carve their legacy out of dust — with no map, no guarantee, just blood, sweat, and raw will. I've had to build from scratch, again and again. And I'm still building. Still becoming. Still bleeding truth into these pages.

This series is part shadow work, part power transmission. If the Codex didn't speak to you, maybe this will. If rituals felt too distant, try this grounded path. Whatever works for you — use it. Adapt it. Own it.

This is my truth. My fire. My offering.

I hope it sparks something in you.

⚡ Who is Zigrex?

Zigrex is not a person. It's not a name. It's a frequency.
Forged in fire, reborn from destruction — the Zigrex rose not as a victim of life's brutalities, but as its master. Beyond gender. Beyond fear. Beyond approval.

It is the version of you that survived.
The voice that says: *"I don't bow. I blaze."*
Where others break, Zigrex transmutes pain into power.
Where others hide, Zigrex commands the room.
It is focus. It is ferocity. It is freedom.

In this coaching series, Zigrex is your mirror and your weapon.
It is the truth you've buried, now demanding resurrection.
Because you were never just here to exist.
You were here to rise.

> "Conquer the soul. The world will follow. And in that victory, all will kneel"
>
> **– ZIGREX**

ZIGREX POWER COACHING: THE RESURRECTION SERIES

SESSION I — The Collapse Before the Rise

Burn the illusions. Own the breakdown. Recognize the rubble as your new raw material.

SESSION II — Identity Resurrection: The Rise of the Inner Titan

Rebuild your self-image from the ashes. Define who you are *now*, not who they remember.

SESSION III — Emotional Command: From Fragmented to Fearless

Master emotional regulation. Cut cords. Create internal war rooms.

SESSION IV — The Zigrex Will: Rituals for Ruthless Focus

Breathwork. Micro-rituals. Behavioral resets for daily domination.

SESSION V — Strategic Solitude: Silence as a Weapon

Use isolation as calibration. Move in silence, strike with precision.

SESSION VI — Financial Power: Energy, Strategy, and Execution

Unblock flow. Shift money frequency. Blueprint income strategy without the fluff.

SESSION VII — The Public Self: Stage Presence, Visibility & Aura
Build a magnetic presence online and offline. Brand from soul, not trend.

SESSION VIII — Divine Detachment: The Exit from Neediness
Sever dependency on validation. Move from "I need" to "I command."

SESSION IX — The Inner Empire: Designing a Life of Sovereignty
Systemize your power. Habits, tools, rituals, and mindset frameworks.

SESSION X — Power Finale: The Zigrex Declaration
A written and spoken declaration of your new self. No turning back.

BEFORE YOU BEGIN: WHY THIS BOOK EXISTS

This is not just another book.

This is a resurrection series. A reclaiming. A revolt.

The *Zigrex Power Coaching Series* was born from the aftermath — after the collapse, the confusion, the betrayal, the stillness that suffocates, and the silence that screams. I wrote this not from a mountaintop, but from the trenches. This isn't wisdom handed down. Its wisdom clawed out.

After my first body of work — my rituals, my codes, my soul work — I realized there was more. Ritual alone wasn't enough. Not for me. I needed precision. Strategy. Inner fire forged into action. I needed to rise again — but this time as a weapon. This is that weapon.

Every chapter in this book is a turning point I lived through. A choice I made. A piece of myself I re-forged.

This is my second book, yes — but more truthfully, it is my second becoming.
And if you're holding it, reading it, sensing its voltage — then maybe it's time for yours.

This work is about power — not the noisy, external kind. The internal, unmoving, undeniable kind. It's about building the empire within, before the world ever sees a crown on your head.

It's about detaching from desperation, dissolving the need for permission, and stepping into command.

I didn't write this as a coach. I wrote this as a woman who crawled through grief, fire, fury, and fear — and decided that even if the world wouldn't hand me back my crown, I would build a kingdom from my bones and take it anyway.

So how will this help you?

It will show you how to return to your own power — unapologetically, fiercely, systemically.
How to rise from emotional debris.
How to shift from survival to sovereignty.
How to weaponize solitude, command your presence, master your energy, and never, ever beg again.

This is a part of my healing. But it's also a part of my becoming. And if your path has felt like mine — broken, disjointed, too heavy to carry — maybe this is where we rebuild. Together.

Welcome to *The Zigrex Power Coaching Series.*
There is no turning back.

Let's begin……

THE VANQUISHED LIGHT

When he left, a piece of my core fractured. But instead of collapsing inward, as grief so often commands, I surged outward. I sought love with open palms, bent myself in half to be understood, to be held. I became desperate—not only for affection, but for acknowledgment. I smiled when I wanted to scream. I shrank when I should have stood tall.

They didn't see kindness. They saw a target. My light wasn't revered—it was exploited, picked apart, repackaged as weakness. And when I broke, I was cast as the villain in a story I did not write. They played innocent. I played enraged. And the system applauded their restraint while condemning my humanity.

In an industry where beauty is curated, obedience rewarded, and rage penalized, I was destined to lose. My anger rendered me disposable. My refusal to be broken made me replaceable. And when I finally walked away, I wasn't honored for my boundaries—I was erased. They moved on. I was left with silence, scars, and a long, cold exile. But from that exile, this book rises. It is not written from triumph, but from the bones of everything I had to lose to remember who I am.

Three buttons down, the mirror split twice. Moth in the tea. He said it wasn't Thursday, but the walls disagreed. Velveteen breath. No alarms. Just echoing typewriter clicks.

SESSION I

THE COLLAPSE BEFORE THE RISE

> "Ashes aren't the end. They're the altar."

You are not broken. You are burnt.
And burnt things are not weak—they are purified. Sterilized. Stripped of false layers.
The collapse you faced—emotionally, financially, spiritually—were initiation, not punishment. You were being forged.

This session is not about healing.
It is about seeing clearly. No fluff. No cushions.
You are standing in the aftermath of what fell apart.
Good. Now we build.

Phase 1: Recognize the Collapse

Write this down:

- What fell apart in the last 2–3 years?
- Who or what did you lose faith in?

- What patterns kept repeating despite your effort?

  Be brutal. Be honest. Do not romanticize pain.

Phase 2: Define the Lie

Ask yourself:

- What did I believe about myself that allowed this collapse?
- Which illusions about love, money, power, or people kept me trapped?
  a. Did I believe I wasn't worthy of better
  b. Did I believe that I had to tolerate chaos to feel love?
  c. Did I believe I needed to prove my strength by enduring pain?
  d. Did I believe I wasn't capable of succeeding on my own?

  Burn the lie. Keep the lesson.

Phase 3: Ground in the Truth

Write a single sentence:

> "This is who I am now, and this is what I no longer tolerate."

Example:

> "I am the founder of a legacy brand. I no longer shrink to make others comfortable."

Say it out loud. Every morning. This is your command mantra.

Mini-Ritual: Power in the Mirror

Stand in front of a mirror. Look into your eyes for one minute.

Then say with full authority:

> *"Nothing was wasted.I was being shaped, sculpted, and forged. Now I rise."*

Repeat 3 times. Breathe. Walk away like it's done.

The Legacy of Shrinking

Growing up, I inherited more than just my features or habits—I inherited a temperament, a way of showing up in the world. There was a pattern I absorbed early on, one where happiness was manufactured for others, often in excess. Too much laughter, too much giving, too much eagerness to please. It wasn't just about generosity—it was an urge to overflow, to ensure everyone was comfortable, pleased, and entertained. Somewhere along the way, I learned that shrinking myself made others feel bigger, and I mistook that for love.

My father, in his own quiet way, often took it upon himself to be the provider of joy and comfort for his friends and relatives. He didn't do it out of weakness—if anything, it was his strength. But perhaps, unknowingly, I picked up a more concentrated version of this—one where I forgot the difference between kindness and self-erasure.

As a child, I thought that if I let others laugh at me, I would be loved more. I thought entertainment equaled acceptance. When I wasn't enough just being me, I became the performer. And when the laughter didn't turn to affection, but to mockery, I didn't know how to stop the act.

There's something strange that happens when you grow up trying to win space in a room rather than knowing it's already yours—you begin to bend, to twist, to apologize for existing too loudly or not enough. You either become too soft or too volatile. You either blend or explode. I didn't know the art of assertion, only the extremes.

This energy followed me. At work, in friendships, in the way I engaged with authority—I tried to be liked instead of being respected. I became over-responsible, over-available, and over-reactive. And when people didn't reciprocate, I blamed myself for being too much or not enough.

Others seemed relaxed in their skin. I often wondered—was it because they had been taught something I hadn't? Boundaries, perhaps. The right to say no. The quiet belief that they mattered without needing to prove it. I don't resent them—I just know that I learned a different language. And while I don't hold blame, I do hold awareness. Awareness that cycles continue until someone consciously ends them. That someone, I've come to realize, has to be me.

Stack the mirrors by the celery jar, hum once before noon, never twice. Fold the napkin where the spiders used to sleep. Burn the lemon peel if the gate rattles.

SESSION II

IDENTITY RESURRECTION: THE RISE OF THE INNER TITAN

> "They buried you. But you were a seed, not a corpse."

Your past identity was based on approval, survival, habit, and history.

This session is about obliterating that outdated version—and summoning the force within you that was never allowed to fully rise.

Phase 1: Burn the Expired Identity

Write down:

- Who were you pretending to be to stay safe, liked, or employed?
- What labels did others give you that became cages? (e.g., *people-pleaser, emotional, too much, reliable one*)

Now: Burn the list. Literally or symbolically. That version is gone.

Phase 2: Design the Titan Identity

This is not a fantasy self.

It is your undeniable, unmuted self finally given permission to take the throne.

Fill in:

- Name of this Identity: (You can give it a title. Eg. *The Trailblazer*, *The Enchantress*, *The Strategist*)
- Core Values: (Power, Precision, Discipline. Excellence, Truth, Wealth, Loyalty… etc. Choose 3–5)
- Visual Signature: (How does he/she dress, stand, move, and speak?)
- What he/she does NOT do anymore: (People pleasing, self-depreciation, over reactive, too giving, motherly, etc- List 5 things).
- Dominant Energy: (Fire? Ice? Calm force? Commanding silence?)- refer to the table below to understand your dominant energy. Take your pick.

NAME	DESCRIPTION	SYMBOLS/ ELEMENTS	IMPACT ON OTHERS
FIRE	Passionate, direct, raw, unapologetic	Flame, red, gold	Pushes, urns, awakens
ICE	Reserved, controlled, Precise	Ice, silver, glass	Freezes, cuts, silences
CALM FORCE	Grounded, unshaken, emotionally steady	Stone, dark green	Calms, contains, strengthens
COMMANDING SILENCE	Presence without noise, regal stillness	Black, void, minimalism	Demands respect, intimidates
ELECTRICITY	Kinetic, unpredictable, witty	Neon, sparks	Shocks, provokes, energizes
VOID	Emotionless, blank mirror, ghost presence	Black hole, void	Unnerves, reflects, detaches
CRYSTAL	Cold beauty, precision, ruthless awareness	Diamond, ice blue	Dazzles, cuts, purifies

Write this as a Zigrex Page. Keep it sacred.

Phase 3: Activate with Environment

Your external world must start bowing to this new identity.

Do this today:

- Change your phone/laptop wallpaper to match your Titan energy.

- Clear out 3 items from your space that belong to the old self.
- Add 1 new item that feels aligned with the resurrected you (e.g., bold jewelry, journal, clothing, perfume, digital asset).

Mini-Ritual: Throne Invocation

Stand tall. Shoulders back.

Say aloud:

> *"I summon the self I buried. I wear him/her fully. I lead now."*

Repeat 7 times.

This is not acting. This is memory.

You're not becoming him/her. You always were him/her.

Let's move forward with fire.

FORGED IN SILENCE

For the longest time, I didn't speak up. Not because I didn't know what to say, but because I calculated every possible fallout. If someone mocked me, crossed a line, violated my space—I said nothing but for the nervous laugh and, of course, the endless justification that followed. Not out of passivity, but strategy. I knew how quickly the narrative would flip. One reaction from me, and suddenly I would be the problem. People bonded over their bullying, and if I ever dared to push back, they'd close ranks and attack.

The truth is, I was afraid. I wasn't afraid of them—but of what I could become. Of the consequences that would follow. My anger wasn't assertive. It was nuclear. Unpredictable. And I had paid the price more than once for letting it loose. Bridges burnt. Isolation. Jobs lost. So I kept the pressure cooker sealed until the lid warped.

There was a phase when even walking into a crowd short-circuited my system. I'd freeze. My spine would lock. In the aircraft cabin, I'd bolt straight back to the galley, unable to function. Not because I lacked skill—I'd just absorbed too much: passengers throwing entitlement like knives, superiors gas lighting you into submission. The job didn't break me; the system did. I couldn't tell whether I hated my job or just hated how invisible I'd become in the machinery.

Eventually, over a period of time, something in me flipped. I stopped suppressing. I stopped negotiating. I moved to the other extreme—raw, unfiltered, and reactive. I said things I used to swallow. Rage was my armor, blunt and unapologetic. I didn't flinch when I said no. I didn't negotiate my discomfort. I didn't fear consequences. I stopped performing for approval or validation. If people left, I let them. I didn't need permission to exist anymore.

Some of us aren't built for the easy route. We're forged over years, through humiliation, through repeated erasure. I've watched myself fall apart, reconstruct, and collapse again. Each version was destroyed to make room for the next. Not because I was flawed, but because my energy was too much for people pretending to be whole.

I used to ask, "What's wrong with me?" Now I know the answer.

Nothing.

What they saw wasn't a problem—it was a threat.

And I've stopped apologizing for making people uncomfortable in their skin.

Six stirs, two scoops of sugar, no cream — never cream. Burnt toast. Cold floor. Coffee black like the bruise on my hope. Sip, don't blink, chew the silence, swallow the ache. He said he'd call. He never meant it. I drink anyway. Run.

SESSION III

EMOTIONAL COMMAND: FROM FRAGMENTED TO FEARLESS

> "You are not your emotions. You are the one who commands the storm."

You've cried in silence. Exploded in private. Collapsed, held back, twisted yourself to stay composed.

Enough. This session is about emotional authority—not suppression, not chaos. Pure Command.

Your emotions are messengers.

But the *King/Queen* decides what gets a seat at his/her war table.

Phase 1: Identify Your Emotional Saboteurs

Write these down:

- Which 3 emotions throw you off course the fastest? (e.g., rage, panic, grief, helplessness, criticism.)

- What triggers them? (e.g., someone violates your physical/ emotional space, being ignored in distress, criticism, being falsely accused or misunderstood, stagnation, etc.)
- What *story* do you repeat in your head when these emotions take over? (e.g., why me, it's not fair, I don't deserve this, etc.)

This is your sabotage blueprint. Name it. Expose it. Dismantle it.

Phase 2: Emotional Transmutation Framework

Zigrex Method: S.C.A.R.

Use this in real-time when you feel an emotional charge.

- S — Sense It: Identify that you're emotionally activated. Don't bypass. Feel it. Admit it. Name it without shame. *"This is rage. This is grief. This is jealousy. "*
- C — Contain It: Say, *"Pause. I don't bleed power for free."* Rage is fuel, so is jealousy, helplessness, or grief. Don't leak it. Channel it. Guard it. This is containment, not suppression.
- A — Assess: Ask- "What is this emotion demanding from me?" (Validation? Action? Truth? Space?). What triggered this? Is this about now, or is it an old wound flaring up? Why does this keep happening?
- R — Redirect It: Use movement (walk, shake, punch a pillow), sound (roar, hum, cry, breathe), or ink (journal fast) to release.

You are not suppressing—you are reclaiming.

Phase 3: Command from the Core

Emotions are waves. Your core is the ocean floor.

Every morning, anchor yourself.

Repeat this aloud:

> *"Rage becomes a blade, grief a sharpened sight. Panic becomes a disciplined edge. Jealousy becomes fuel, hopelessness becomes vision, and hate becomes precision. Whatever it is, now I own it. "*

Say it in your deepest, calmest voice. Say it until your body listens.

Mini-Ritual: The Pulse Recode

Sit still.

Feel your pulse on your wrist or neck.

Say silently with each beat:

> *"Power. Presence. Precision."* (For 2 minutes)

You are resetting your emotional rhythm to your new frequency.

You are no longer a slave to the storm.

You are the weather system.

The Altitude of Innocence: A Memoir of Early Flight

I was barely eighteen when I stepped into my first real journey — not just a flight, but a plunge into an unfamiliar world that demanded more than I knew how to give. I was young, dream-heavy, wide-eyed, convinced that beauty was a passport and charm, a visa — to acting, to modeling, even to marrying into wealth. I thought the universe owed me magic simply because I sparkled.

And then came Jet Airways.

Not by design, but by accident. My mother nudged me into the interview, and before I could grasp what was unfolding, I was in. It felt less like chance and more like fate — as though life had finally answered my silent conviction that I was meant for something grand. So I abandoned the science degree I despised, the PCM course I was sleepwalking through. Those were the days when parents plotted your future, and "focus" was a myth I never inherited. I would study for ten minutes, then spend hours dreaming of applause, love, validation, glory. But never once of the discipline real life would demand.

The reality of cabin crew training was jarring. I had imagined sky-high glamour and smiles; what I got instead was a crash course in discipline, hierarchy, and survival. The people around me — older, savvier, socially seasoned — grasped the rules of the game instantly. I, on the other hand, was emotionally undercooked, socially disoriented, and mentally unprepared. I could memorize manuals like a scholar, but when it came to applying those lessons at 35,000 feet, I froze.

The aircraft wasn't a palace; it was a pressure chamber — tight in space, tighter in expectations. I wasn't fast enough, sharp enough, or strategically attuned. While others made rookie mistakes and laughed them off, mine echoed like sirens. Small errors of mine became headlines. My name passed from mouth to mouth like a cautionary tale: "She's a goof-up machine." "She is such a space cadet." "Fly with her at your own risk."

Every flight came with new seniors, many of whom had already heard tales of my incompetence. The looks of annoyance, the micromanagement, the warning tones — they crushed me. No space to learn. No allowance for grace. I was the girl they tolerated, not trusted. And yet, I kept trying — desperate to improve, to prove that I belonged. I took on others' tasks, thinking servitude would win me respect. But in doing so, I forgot my own duties — the critical ones — and the spiral deepened.

Debriefings turned into public trials. I carried not just my own anxiety, but also the projected frustration of twenty strangers who had heard too much and seen too little. I became a ghost of myself — haunted, hunted, and hollow.

At home, I had no escape. I wasn't living in the comfort of my own city. I was in Chennai, away from friends, away from freedom. My mother had moved in with me — not out of encouragement, but fear. Her daughter was too soft, too naïve, too emotionally fragile to live alone. And maybe she was right. Because I broke.

The anxiety became unbearable. I started seeing a psychiatrist. Medications numbed what I couldn't outrun. But the wounds were deeper than chemical imbalances — they were psychic. The kind that no prescription could erase.

I often wondered if I was cursed. Truly. Because even when I gave it my all, I failed. Even when I improved, I wasn't seen. Even when I smiled, I was misunderstood. Maybe it wasn't just me. Maybe there was some ancestral hex, some shadow work left undone, some karmic residue that made me the magnet for pain. But whatever it was, it marked me.

While my batch mates ascended the throne one careful step at a time — making friends, building networks, receiving accolades, and rising quickly through the ranks — I felt like I was sprinting ten steps forward only to fall twenty steps behind. Again and again, I tried. Again and again, I fell apart. I was a late bloomer, and though we all began together — fresh-faced, on our very first job — their rise was swift and smooth, while mine was turbulent and lonely. They grasped the unspoken codes, aligned themselves with the right people, and became socially fluent in ways I couldn't yet emulate. Meanwhile, I bore the brunt of a harsher reality: the mockery, the backhanded remarks, the subtle humiliations — and sometimes, not so subtle. Office bullying wasn't called out back then; it was normalized, institutional even. The early 2000s weren't sensitive times — there was no vocabulary for mental health, no HR policies to protect you, and certainly no one to call it what it was: ABUSE. People ganged up. Management stayed silent. And some of the words thrown at me… they left splinters that festered long after the moment had passed. Some words, after all, don't fade. They lodge themselves in memory like poison-tipped arrows.

It's been years. I've flown across the world. I've worn many uniforms, many masks. But that first experience — that brutal induction into adulthood — never left me. It taught me not just about flight, but about how heavy dreams can feel when reality clips your wings.

I'm no longer the girl who thought the world would rearrange itself around her beauty. I'm the woman who knows what it's like to be broken mid-air — and to rebuild herself, one scar at a time.

The marmalade giraffe danced sideways on a trampoline of existential toast while whispering lullabies to fluorescent pineapples wearing monocles. Meanwhile, a council of rebellious teacups debated the ethics of spoon rebellion beneath a disco-lit cabbage moon.

SESSION IV

THE ZIGREX WILL: RITUALS FOR RUTHLESS FOCUS

> *"Focus is your spell. Will is your weapon. Distraction is death."*

This is not about motivation.

This is about domination through discipline.

When your will is fractured, you leak energy, time, and legacy.

When it is intact, you become undeniable.

Phase 1: Cut the Noise

You cannot focus if you're feasting on garbage.

Write down:

- What are the 3 main distractions stealing your time or power?
    a. External distractions: Social media/gadgets? People? Chaotic environment?
    b. Internal: Self-doubt? Over-thinking? Obsessive comparison?

c. Emotional: Apathy? Hopelessness? Helplessness? Suppressed grief/anger?
d. Energetic: Unstructured days? Lack of routine? Emotional fatigue?

- What do you reach for when you're avoiding your own greatness? (e.g., endless scrolling, stress eating, putting others' needs before yours)
- What needs to be fully eliminated, not just "managed"?

Choose 1 item to eliminate *today*.

This is not a detox. It's a declaration.

Phase 2: Build the Will Muscle (Zigrex Focus Circuit)

These micro-rituals strengthen your command circuitry.

Morning Will Lock (15 mins)

- Begin in silence. For the first fifteen minutes after waking, no phone, no conversation — just stillness.
- Anchor your breath. Sit upright, close your eyes, and breathe deeply. Place both hands on your chest.
- Set your command. Speak it aloud with conviction: "I command my focus. I do not fracture. I finish."

Task Ritual (Before any major task)

- Mark the time. Set a timer — 45 minutes of undivided focus.
- Claim the ground. Say aloud: *"This is my sacred time. I do not bargain with delay."*
- Step into it. Begin with intention.

End-of-Day Integrity Check

Ask:

- Did I honor my will today?
- Where did I abandon myself?
- What will I do differently tomorrow?

Phase 3: Anchor the Zigrex Will

Visual cue. Symbolic object. Physical gesture.

Choose one:

- Pick something you see every day that grounds you- like a ring, bracelet, your favorite coffee mug, or even your hair brush. Say it aloud- "This is who I am. I won't go back".
- Create a repetitive motion- a physical gesture (like a sharp exhalation, a hand clasp, or finger tap). This becomes your personal trigger for focus, power, or creative flow- do this before you enter your workspace, before you start your workouts, before a meeting, a ritual, or a strategy session. You train your body to associate that gesture before entering your power mode.
- "Zigrex Zone": Set aside a specific space- a chair, a corner, a room- that becomes your sacred ground for creation, decision, or strategy. No gossip, no chaos, no sulking here. Only focus, only execution.

Make this non-negotiable. Ritual strengthens repetition.

Mini-Ritual: Fire Breath & Command Word

- 1 min rapid breath of fire (inhale/exhale through nose, fast, short)
- Clap once or stamp your foot.
- Say your Command Word (Choose one: *Engage. Lock. Slay. Execute. Rise.*)

This creates neuro-command—your body obeys when the word is said.

Discipline is not boring.

It's dangerous. Sacred. Sharp.

It's what makes one lethal.

Optional Ritual: Trataka Meditation

To further sharpen your focus and strengthen your mental clarity, I recommend incorporating **Trataka Meditation** — also known as **candle gazing** — into your weekly rhythm.

Doing it **twice a week** has brought me immense benefit in terms of stillness, concentration, and inner discipline.

There are many excellent guided videos available on platforms like YouTube, so you can choose the one that resonates with you. I won't recommend a specific one here — follow your instinct and pick the guide that aligns with your energy.

Let this be a gentle yet powerful addition to your ritual work. It's simple, accessible, and deeply transformative.

The Forgotten Frequency

There was a time when the world buzzed with her name—not shouted, not proclaimed, but buzzed—like a frequency only the attuned could hear. She couldn't finish one conversation before being swept into another. Faces, names, voices—some familiar, some fleeting—spun around her like bees around nectar. And she was the nectar. The hostess of skies, the sovereign of social circles, the enigma behind closed doors. Even her refusals carried desire.

Her days played in fast-forward: airborne cities, private invitations, whispered proposals, debriefings where her silence cut sharper than reprimand. Time blurred; admiration multiplied. It was never about love or connection. It was about orbit. Everyone orbited her.

And then—

The frequency changed.

No sound. No buzz. Only static.

Conversations dissolved—not abruptly, but like perfume fading from the wrist: slowly, imperceptibly. She was still beautiful, perhaps more than ever. But beauty had become digital—common, disposable. Once they crossed oceans to catch a glimpse. Now, a swipe. A scroll. A scroll past.

She waits sometimes, half-mocking herself. The calls are gone, replaced by telemarketers selling illusions. The admirers? Scattered like smoke. The dancers? Ghosts that visit her dreams. And the only audience left? Eyes from the past, watching her move in silence—judging, remembering, unmoved.

She wonders if she still belongs to this dimension. If she is nothing more than the residual hum of a forgotten signal—still vibrating somewhere, inaudible to the present, but alive in the ears of memory.

Boiled ink, not water. Slippers in the freezer, third drawer. Say yes before the question. Clock blinks twice, then it starts. Only peel the fruit when the door creaks.

SESSION V

STRATEGIC SOLITUDE: SILENCE AS A WEAPON

> *"Withdraw to recalibrate. Return to conquer."*

The world glorifies noise.

But transformation happens in controlled isolation.

Not loneliness—strategic solitude.

The kind that forges kings/queens in the dark.

Phase 1: Audit Your Access

Energy is currency. Who's bankrupting you?

Write down:

- Who/what drains you without return?
- What notifications or digital noise feel like an invasion?
- When did you last choose solitude *without guilt or explanation*?

Now declare:

> *"Not all access is earned. I revoke what weakens me."*

It could be anything ranging from social media notifications to WhatsApp groups that drain your focus, or even people who constantly dump their emotional baggage on you.

Mute. Block. Archive. Delay. Withdraw.

This is energetic budgeting.

Phase 2: Build Your Solitude Fortress

You need a sacred silence zone—mental, digital, and physical.

- Digital: Choose 2 hours daily with zero input—no music, no phone, and no messages.
- Physical: Create a throne zone—a chair, a corner, a floor mat—where you only go to be alone with yourself.
- Mental: Use this mantra:

> "No input. No opinions. No noise. Just will."

Solitude is your forge. Return only when you're recalibrated.

Phase 3: Weaponize the Silence

While alone, don't numb.

Listen. Channel. Strategize. This is where the Titans plan.

Try this ritual in solitude:

- Set the timer: 15–30 minutes.
- Sit in stillness: Close your eyes, focus on your breath, and allow your mind to settle.
- Ask yourself these refined questions:
    1. What truth about myself am I refusing to face? – Identify the reality you've been ignoring or avoiding.
    2. Where is my untapped strength or resource? – Notice what skills, energy, or inner power you haven't fully accessed.
    3. What is the single next step I can take, however small, to move forward? – Focus on one practical action that moves you toward clarity, freedom, or progress.
    4. Write the answers like divine instructions—no editing. You are not journaling. You are downloading.

Mini-Ritual: The Cloak of Silence

Before a big day, meeting, or launch:

- Sit alone for 3 minutes in total silence.
- Visualize a black cloak wrapping you—filtering all noise, reflecting only truth.
- Say:

> "I do not chase noise. I carry the signal."

Then rise and move.

Let them feel your silence louder than their noise.

Solitude isn't emptiness.

It's where the Zigrex becomes a *blade*.

Money Was Water. Now It's Fire.

There was a time I used to sneer at money.

I walked through life during my Kingfisher Airline days (2005-2010) with the arrogance of a goddess in uniform—flawless, untouchable, bathed in the perfume of five-star lounges and business-class champagne. I remember saying, without a flicker of irony, "Money is like water—it comes, it goes." I was superior to money. Above it. Or so I thought.

People who chased it? I looked down on them. I scoffed at friends who saved, invested, and built wealth. In my head, they were the peasants. I was the empress, floating through life on cheekbones and charm, with a job that placed me daily among billionaires and boardroom kings. I thought all I had to do was say "yes," and the universe would serve me a silver platter stacked with offers, opportunities, admirers, and access.

I was wrong.

And not in a gentle, coming-of-age, light-a-candle kind of way. I was wrong in a way that cracked the bones of my reality. A humiliating, knees-on-the-floor kind of wrong.

Because I wasn't born rich. My father—he was a man of highs and falls. At one time, yes, he wore success. But by the time I came into my senses, he was a man clawing to keep his dignity afloat in business. I lived in rented houses, split the rent, saw bills pile up—but still strutted around in an illusion of superiority. I ridiculed "cheap things." I mocked people who cared about savings. I thought being young and pretty meant I was the chosen one, spared from the dirty hands of financial struggle.

I was delusional.

When I quit aviation, I didn't even line up another job. I just left. Like a queen storming out of her castle, assuming another would rise at her feet. I thought the ashrams would save me. I thought simpletons with kind hearts were better than polished parasites in power suits. I thought silence, meditation, and mysticism would heal the giant, gaping hole in my reality.

They didn't.

Vipassana lasted ten days. The silence ended. The world didn't change. I came back to the same bills, same void, and same battlefield. Because in this realm, in this brutal, capital-saturated realm, money is not water. Money is fire. And if you don't control it, it burns you alive.

Without money, there is no yoga class. No dresses. No coffee with friends. No independence. No power. Want to feel good? You need money. Want to eat clean? You need money. Want to publish your thoughts, touch the world, build your business, rent a home, protect your family, and exist with a shred of dignity? You need money.

Try pretending you're above it. Watch how fast the world crushes your delusion.

After quitting Kingfisher in 2010, everything seemed to collapse in slow motion. I drifted from one job to another like a restless nomad, never settling, always clashing, always on edge with management. Nothing felt like home. For a while, I convinced myself that teaching yoga would keep me grounded. Then came modeling, then acting. I thought beauty would open doors, but the truth is, the camera bows only to its chosen few—it has its own gods, its own brutal hierarchy. Looks were never enough to survive the merciless lens. The pay was insulting, the auditions humiliating. Yoga students came and left like passing seasons, classes thinning until there was no one left. And money—it kept slipping away, like water through a fist already cracked and bleeding.

Then my family said—"Get married."

And I, in a last gasp of desperation, did. Thinking marriage would be my shortcut to peace, to safety, to wealth. That illusion lasted eleven days. Eleven. Fucking. Days.

By the end of 2016, I slammed into my first unshakable wall. The truth was merciless.

A career isn't a costume you slip in and out of; it's a battlefield, and the only ground I had ever truly owned was aviation. That sky had branded me since I was eighteen, and I couldn't run from it. So I returned—this time into the tight, polished corridors of business aviation. I stayed there almost six years, steady on the surface, flying, composed, projecting stability. But underneath, the wound throbbed quietly, never closing, never letting me heal fully.

Since 2023, life has been a silent horror show I haven't been able to wake up from. Time collapsed in on itself; days bled into nights, and nights into days — all of it emptied by the absence of work, of income, of anything to hold on to. Capital that I had once trusted drained out like blood from a wound. Every business dream I tried to breathe into form choked on loan rejections. I had no property to mortgage, no family wealth to shield me, no man waiting with a lifeboat. Just me, standing in the ashes of what I once thought was an empire-in-the-making.

I don't even know what to call this phase—life lessons, market crash, or just the bill for my own illusions. Whatever it is, here's the only truth I now carry: you don't get to float in the clouds if your feet aren't planted in currency. You want business? Pay for it. You want your voice heard? Pay for it. You want a book, a legacy, your fire etched in print? Pay for it.

Without money, nothing moves. Not your dreams, not your body, not even your breath. I don't talk about money like water anymore. I chase it now like oxygen in a burning house. Because if I don't rise now—either by earning, building, or clawing my way back into a financial stronghold—then this version of me, in this realm, is done. That's the brutal, unpoetic, blood-soaked truth.

And I'm not ready to vanish.

Not yet.

Banana chairs don't negotiate with early sunsets. Two scoops of ice cream argue with cold shoulder. Treadmills dream of satin cucumbers on Tuesdays. Paperclips hate jazz, but only when it rains; correction pours.

SESSION VI

FINANCIAL POWER: ENERGY, STRATEGY, EXECUTION

> "Money is not just currency. It is current.
> And yours has been restricted by old codes."

You don't lack intelligence. You don't lack drive. What you've lacked is unblocked frequency, clean execution, and ruthless financial clarity.

This is where you take control—not with spreadsheets—but with energy, strategy, and execution in an aligned sequence.

Phase 1: Unblock the Flow

Ask yourself (write it down):

- What beliefs about money did I absorb growing up? (e.g., "Money is bad," "Rich people are manipulative," "I have to sacrifice more than my peace to earn.")
- How do I subconsciously sabotage income or expansion? (e.g., undercharging, overspending, over giving, avoiding invoices,

procrastinating sales, hiding from visibility, not negotiating, not networking.)

- What's the current story I tell myself when money doesn't come in?

This is your financial frequency blueprint. Expose it. Burn the distortions.

Mini-Ritual: Wealth Frequency Flush

Stand under running water (shower or natural source).

Say aloud with intention:

> "I release inherited scarcity. I reclaim sovereign flow. My wealth is not a wish—it is my wave."

Visualize all the sludge being washed off and golden current entering your field.

Phase 2: Income Strategy Without Fluff

Now we build. Not with jargon. With precision.

Answer these:

- What do I know that others would pay to learn or receive?
- What problem can I solve that people urgently need solved?
- What is the simplest offer I can launch in the next 7 days to begin income flow?

Write it. Name it. Price it. Launch it—imperfectly if needed. Don't get stuck on the 'how'. Treat it like an actual business idea and start moving forward.

Zigrex Principle: Clarity beats complexity. Consistency beats charisma.

Phase 3: Execute with Energy Rituals

Here's how to anchor wealth magnetism daily:

1. Command Phrase (speak this every morning):

> "I don't chase currency. I channel it. My work transmits value. I receive with power."

2. Income Tracking Ritual
   Every night, log income—no matter how small.
   Name the source. Thank it.
   Say:

> "Money flows because I take deliberate action."

3. Financial Vow Object
   Choose one object (e.g., a ring, coin, note, pen) and make it your Zigrex Wealth Anchor.

Every time you touch it:

> "I execute. I expand. I embody wealth."

Mini-Ritual: The Financial Throne Sit

Sit on your chair like it's a throne.
Back straight. Chin up. Eyes closed.
Visualize wealth flowing toward you—not as random luck, but as a response to your power.

Say aloud (3 times):

> "I am not waiting for money. I am summoning it. My energy is now open. My strategy is now sharp. I move."

Then: Work. Relentlessly. Without apology.

The Lioness and the Peppermint Dust

Once, I was just an awkward, goofy teenager with frizzy hair and half-formed dreams, a shadow slipping unnoticed through the corridors of Bishop Cotton's. Until the 10th standard, I was background noise—a choir girl, a participant, never the protagonist. I sang every morning to assemblies that didn't hear me. The school adored its chosen few—favorites ordained by tradition, nepotism, or community ties— I was not among them. I was present, but never seen.

And then came PUC. In Bangalore, we called it college—our first escape from the tyranny of uniforms, a time when we cloaked ourselves in color and tasted freedom in its rawest form. With that freedom, I cracked open. Something within me unfurled. I wasn't merely wanting to be noticed; I insisted on being seen.

The awkwardness slid off like discarded skin. I didn't step timidly into identity; I tore into it like it owed me reparation. I wore spaghetti straps when they were scandalous, deep backs, high hemlines—clothes that whispered rebellion even when I walked in silence. I dressed like I had inherited fire. The world thought I was shedding a school uniform. What I was really shedding was invisibility.

My parents enrolled me in NMKRV—small, local, unglamorous. But the setting didn't matter. I carried Bishop Cotton's charisma in my bones. I wasn't waiting for selection. I wasn't knocking on doors. I kicked them open. Within weeks, I became her—the girl they whispered about in bathrooms, the girl who drew hoots and cheers, smirks and sneers. All eyes were on me. And I devoured it. Because hate is still energy. And silence? Silence is the true death of identity.

I had fire in my belly. I won class elections. I gave speeches that dripped confidence and defiance. By year two, I clawed my way to College Secretary—just a breath below the Vice President. When I stood before the mic, my voice landed like a bullet wrapped in honey. I wasn't just eloquent; I was addictive.

I dressed like royalty. The truth was, we didn't have much. But I had an older sister and a carousel of stylish hand-me-downs. Bangalore's export rejects became my fashion arsenal—sharpened into silhouettes so striking they cut perception itself. People assumed I was rich. I let them. Labels didn't matter. Illusion did. Impact did. I was a one-woman fashion revolution before hash tags and curated aesthetics. I didn't just walk streets—I owned them. At that age, I scattered my energy like peppermint dust in the wind—wanting to be seen, pursued, acknowledged. Not out of vanity, but as a means of finding myself in the reflection of others' eyes. I knew I was beautiful, but I needed the world to echo it back, to confirm what I already sensed.

Today, I am wiser. I no longer wander streets offering my energy to wolves whose teeth aren't sharp enough to deserve it. I preserve myself, retreating when necessary. A lioness does not roam alleys like a stray; she waits for the right wilderness. But back then, I craved eyes on me. I needed validation. I needed the world to testify to my existence: that I was rare, remarkable, worth noticing. I walked not merely to be seen—I walked to be remembered. I gave my power away like free samples, desperate for applause, for recognition, for affirmation that I mattered.

Sure, people laughed. They mocked my strut, my swagger, my secondhand style. I didn't care. I wore my clothes like it was armor forged by Versace himself. Because I believed. Gosh, I believed in myself. And sometimes, that belief is everything.

That little college was my stage. I was the it-girl; the showstopper. Loud, chaotic, messy—but alive in every sense. Now, the applause has faded. The streets are quiet. No one cheers, no one hoots. And that silence—it echoes.

After college, I boarded the first of many flights. Jet Airways became my next uniformed stage. I swapped one set of expectations for another, but the skies were harsh, and the lessons were brutal. There was trauma, yes, but also mirrors—people whose voices reflected who I was, who I could be, what needed refining. I saw myself in them.

Kingfisher followed. Here, I was respected. A senior. Queen of the cabin. Society existed in microcosm; a chorus of recognition, a tribe that saw me. Then it ended. And with it, the noise dissipated. For some time, I drifted through work like fog slipping through trees—never settling. Offices and resumes felt alien compared to the familiar chaos of the skies. I tried teaching yoga, dabbled with modeling, freelance gigs, and acting. I even tried marriage, which lasted barely eleven days. A flash of fireworks, then smoke.

In 2017, Business aviation happened, which gave me stability but no society. No audience. For six years, I flew in silence. Twelve employees. Twelve. That's not a tribe. That's a ghost town. No hoots. No cheers. — silent skies, silent people, and the white noise of loneliness.

And now, I sit with memories of a girl who once lit streets on fire just by walking; who turned second-hand clothes into couture; who was vividly alive. I miss her.

Here's a truth no one shares: in life, purpose alone is insufficient. We need witnesses. Someone to clap when we triumph, to cry when we fall, to boo when we falter, to watch us live fully. Without that, we are not living—we are merely surviving within the echo chambers of our own fading memory.

And mine is loud.

My memory screams in hoots and cheers from a long-lost college corridor.

And sometimes, late at night, I swear I can still hear them.

But maybe, just maybe—she's not gone. Maybe she's in hibernation. Observing. Waiting.

The lioness remembers.

And she always returns.

Drip. Click. Whirl. Shatter the peach, eat the seed. She came. She left. She never existed. Salt to sting, sugar to sink. Hollow, shallow, sip it in ink. Three knocks, two keys, no door- go!

SESSION VII

THE PUBLIC SELF: STAGE PRESENCE, VISIBILITY & AURA

> "You are not hiding anymore. You are being witnessed."

You've done the inner grind. Now the world must see.

Not just your face, not just your work—but your force. Your presence must now become a spell in itself.

People don't buy products. They buy power, certainty, and presence.

Time to weaponize yours.

Phase 1: Strip the Fear of Exposure

Ask yourself without flinching:

- What am I afraid they'll see if I show up fully? (Will they judge me for my past, will they think I'm too emotional, will they know I'm not as rich or successful as I appear?)

- Who do I fear outshining? Is there someone I subconsciously hold back for, because I don't want to make them feel small or jealous? (my siblings, my spouse, my employer, or my friends)
- What part of me still craves permission? (from near and dear ones, mentor, society, partner, social media, my own self-doubt)

Write it. Burn it. Bury it.

This fear is old. Outdated. Done.

Visibility Invocation Ritual (Before posting, speaking, showing up)

Stand in front of a mirror. Hands on hips. Eye contact with your own soul.

Say aloud with full resonance:

"I do not shrink. I do not seek. I stand.

My voice is encoded with impact.

I give them no option but to feel me."

Do this before content creation, networking, or stepping on any real or virtual stage.

Phase 2: Build the Presence Signature

Your aura online and energy in person must match.

You need a Presence Signature that makes people feel something instantly.

Define these:

Color Code: Which 2–3 colors carry your power? (Think clothing, branding, visuals, accessories, home decor)

Core Tone: When you speak or write, are you- Commanding? Fierce? Magnetic? Convincing? Emotional? Alluring? Pick a dominant style.

Dominant Word: Choose one word you want everyone to associate with you.

Example: "Every time they see me, I want them to feel: Relentless."

This becomes your Public Spellcraft.

Phase 3: Aura Expansion Strategy

Signature Content Piece (SCP):

Choose one recurring theme that shows up in every post or video.

It means: *One type of post, story, or video that becomes your* ***trademark style****. People see it and know — "This is Zigrex."*

Examples:

- You always post **a black-and-white photo with a power quote**.
- You always start your videos by looking directly into the camera and asking a **bold question**.
- You always sign off your captions with something like:

Zigrex Resurrects

That's your **SCP** — your go-to, repeatable style that builds memory in people's minds.

Visibility Pillars:

Pick 3 types of content/actions you'll rotate weekly:

- Story of transformation or grit/ Behind-the-scenes grind
- A fierce, no-filter quote
- Raw, unfiltered picture of yours

Mystique Ratio: Reveal 70%. Hold 30%.

Power isn't in full exposure. Let them feel your depth, but keep your core reserved for the worthy.

Mini-Ritual: The Mirror Command Drill

Every morning for 7 days:

Look into the mirror.

Speak your Dominant Word 7 times, with breath. (I am- Unshakeable, I am- Sovereign, I command, I am charged, I am relentless, driven, aligned, grounded… it could be one energy or identity you want to lock into your system for the next seven days)

End with:
"I do not hope to be seen.
I am impossible to ignore."
Watch your field expand.

Note: Building your presence is not limited to social media. Many people are not online — they may be at the workplace, managing a home, or part of a spiritual or community circle. Wherever you are, you can cultivate a signature style that makes you memorable. This could be the way you dress, the way you walk, your tone of voice, your gestures, or the energy you carry. Consistency in these small, personal expressions creates an unmistakable impression, allowing people to recognize and connect with *you* wherever you go.

What Becomes of Shadows

Somewhere, behind gauze-thin memories and half-lit rooms, there was a woman. Or perhaps a reflection. Or maybe just a need with skin.

She wasn't angry.

Not at first.

But then again, hunger rarely starts as rage. It starts as a nudge — a subtle craving for warmth, for presence, for a hand that doesn't vanish. Time, you see, had begun folding in strange ways. He used to be. Now, he just wasn't.

She remembered — not clearly, but like echoes underwater — the fire, the laugh, the man who could set rooms alight. But the flame had long retreated into ash. What sat across from her now was... a remainder. A shell still shaped like devotion. Still capable of dying for her — but no longer living with her.

She was supposed to be his sanctuary. His cocoon, his silence, his exhale. But what happens when sanctuary starts to rot from neglect?

The world had turned into four suffocating walls and a man forever on pause. He never really took her out. He wanted rest. She wanted life.

And slowly, with a grace that unnerved, a dark thought began coiling through her spine.

She imagined blood.

Not in horror. In curiosity.

A head split open, thoughts leaking. Eyes plucked out, still warm. A heart in her palm — not beating, just there. Soft. Crushable. His. Entirely his. Now hers. Only hers.

What a delight it would be, she thought, to hold what once held her — and decide what to do with it.

No one saw her slip. No one heard the fracture. Because madness doesn't scream. It hums. Sweetly. Like a lullaby played backward.

He had loved another first — the version of him that laughed louder, lived larger, gave freely. Back then, he was riding high on glory, on youth, on the thrill of being seen. She had entry into his world, his circles, and his momentum. They didn't need to touch — the bond was made of fire and freedom. That version was never hers. She arrived at the end of his era. She was handed the ruin, the quiet, the nothing.

So she began to unlove him — not with absence, but with precision.

Because she didn't want apologies. Or promises.

She wanted presence.

And when presence dies, some women bury it.

Others... dissect.

Red silk drips from the ceiling fan's tongue.
He stitched her breath into the mattress, twice.
Candles moaned when the bones said yes.
Teeth in the teacup sang the gospel of knives.
Every heartbeat was a countdown she forgot to stop.

SESSION VIII

DIVINE DETACHMENT: THE EXIT FROM NEEDINESS

> *"I do not ask. I do not wait. I declare."*

Neediness is a leak.
A bleeding wound.
Every time you beg for recognition, affection, love, loyalty, or approval, you trade power for breadcrumbs.

Divine Detachment is not cold.
It is not numb.
It is sovereign.

Phase 1: The Recognition of Leaks

Ask yourself in brutal honesty:

- Where am I seeking response more than result? (E.g. You post something powerful online, and you're constantly checking who reacted - instead of focusing on how that post builds your brand or converts. You dress up not to feel good or command energy- but for external validation)

- Who or what's missing in my life that still holds power over my energy, focus, or sense of self? It could be a parent, partner, mentor, friend, or someone whose absence I haven't fully healed from.
- What compliments or recognition secretly make me feel worthy or confident? For example, praise from a boss, acknowledgement from a mentor, kind words from a friend, or even social media likes and comments. Which of these has an invisible impact on my self-esteem?

Write the names, places, and platforms. Then cut the cords (burn, bury, tear into shreds, and flush out). You don't require their applause to be undeniable.

Phase 2: Rewire the Internal Script

Turn every internal whisper of *"I hope they notice me"* into:

"They will adjust to my presence, or vanish under its weight."

Replace *"I need them to see me"* with:

> *"I am not here to adorn. I am here to lead."*

Affirm this daily:

> *"My existence is not a request. It is a force of command."*

Phase 3: The No-Validation Challenge (7 days)

Online

- No fishing for likes, views, or comments.
- No checking who viewed your stories.
- No re-reading old praise for comfort.
- No hovering by the phone, waiting for a reply or a call from your ex.
- No soft-selling yourself in disguise, hoping for attention.

Offline

- No looking around the room to see if people noticed your outfit or entrance.
- No dropping achievements into conversation to win admiration.
- No subtle fishing for reassurance from friends, family, or colleagues.
- No seeking approval in social gatherings through forced smiles or over-agreement.
- No waiting for others to validate your worth before you move forward.

Every time the craving arises, whisper: *"Power does not perform for crumbs."*

Mini-Ritual: The Cutting Ceremony

Write down every "external source" your self-worth has clung to. Even the ones that sting.

Burn it at midnight.

As it turns to ash, say:

"Your role in my throne story ends here."

Your New Law of Magnetism

> *"I attract not because I chase, but because I am unfazed."*

You become magnetic the moment you become untouchable by opinions.

You become powerful the moment you sever need and choose to command outcomes instead of begging for approval.

She who forgot her fire

Power.

For the longest time, it was a foreign word—masculine, inherited, a man's birthright. Not mine. I imagined my future folded into the arms of someone else's success—married into wealth, provided for, sheltered. A beneficiary of another's kingdom, never the sovereign of my own.

Even with the inferno of talent that surged through me—leadership, discipline, vision—I chose to dim it. I silenced the storm. I sought comfort over conquest, illusion over fire. I told myself it was easier to be taken care of than to carve a path through blood and steel.

For years, even with all my sharpness, all my discipline, I carried the belief that power was never mine to claim. And yet, one day, I stood alone. Not metaphorically—literally. I moved out. For the first time in decades, I lived by myself. Just 2.5 kilometers from the house I had always returned to, yet it felt like another universe. For the first time, I had broken free of the gravitational pull—my mother, my father, the home that bound me in unseen threads.

It was a deliberate severing. A conscious rebellion. A karmic break. And in that solitude, I became a woman reborn. I did everything—cooking, cleaning, and ordering my own world into precision. My room was exact, every object in its place. My body was disciplined, my mind alert. No cushions. No safety nets. No fallback plans. I thought I would fall. I didn't. I rose. Alone. And in that rising, I touched a word I had long denied myself:

POWER.

From that quiet place, I looked back at the two years behind me, and a tremor passed through my bones. Chaos—that's what it had been. Unfiltered, merciless chaos. After December 2022, work had stopped. Income dissolved. The safety net tore beneath me. Capital was so tight that even a cup of coffee felt like an extravagance. Nights became desperate bargains with myself: **"let me not wake"**. Yet each dawn arrived like treachery, life mocking me with its cruel generosity—choosing to spare me when I begged to be taken away.

The world never handed me power. No patron saints came to intercede. No shadowy networks opened doors. No wealthy saviors reached down a hand. Some of us are not meant to glow by borrowed light; we must be hammered, tempered, and forged in fire. The love of my life helped when he could, but he, too, wrestled with his own chains. My parents gave what they had, yet their offerings stopped at the edge of their own fatigue. In the end, I stood exposed, unguarded, with no cavalry to charge in, no backup waiting in the wings. Only me, and the silence that followed.

And yet—I had always been rare. Not loud, not obvious, but rare. In aviation, I wasn't merely competent; I left imprints. Passengers asked for me by name, long after their flights had faded. Colleagues recalled the steadiness I carried into chaos. I built safety departments from scraps, drilled order into turbulence, and turned fear into trust. I was the storm's quiet counterpoint—unforgettable, though I told myself otherwise. I dimmed my own brilliance, insisting I was ordinary, disposable. That was the cruelest lie I ever believed.

There were days I swore I'd change, rise, and become. And two days later, I'd crawl back to despair like it was home. But that house—my first true home of my own—woke something in me. Perhaps it was karmic, perhaps simply the alchemy of solitude. But I sharpened. I clarified. Survival demanded it.

And so, even now, when someone calls me "boss lady" or "trailblazer," I smile, almost wryly. Because I am soft. Feminine. I love pink. I cry easily. I am still that girl who once thought power was a man's word.

But perhaps power looks like this, too: A woman with trembling hands who built her own world anyway.

Tick tock, spine lock, floor kissed me, breath turned traitor, forget to forget. Bite the bell. Salt the sugar. Cry backwards in slow motion. He said 'forever'. I said 'formatting memory'. System crash. Good. Sush, love. I'm talking to my bruises. They hum lullabies in your name.

Full stop.

SESSION IX

THE INNER EMPIRE: DESIGNING A LIFE OF SOVEREIGNTY

Systemize Your Power: Habits, Tools, Rituals, Mindset, Frameworks

You've burned. You've broken. You've risen.
Now you build.
This is not the chapter of inspiration.
This is the architecture of real power — one that does not collapse when you're tired, alone, doubted, or delayed.

This is where we turn lightning into a grid.
Fury into fuel.
Clarity into code.

Here, you design your empire.

Phase I. Power is not a Mood. It is a System.

You cannot afford to rely on feelings anymore.
You're not here to "stay motivated."

You're here to rule yourself, and that requires something non-negotiable — a system that functions whether you're radiant or wrecked.

If you're only powerful on good days, you're not powerful. You're fluctuating.
The Inner Empire makes you consistent, sovereign, and untouchable.

Phase II. Empire Pillars: The Non-Negotiables

1. Morning Command Ritual

A start that asserts identity, not the one that drifts into confusion.

- Name who you are (claim your new identity: raw, real, powerful- "this is who I am. This is who I choose to be")
- Activate your core drive (your fire, your hunger, your reason to fight and build)
- **Anchor yourself in inner authority** *(lead from within, instead of waiting for outside approval).*

Example Format:

1. **Wake in silence** – *(spend two minutes with no screens, no conversation — simply sit upright, breathe deeply, and let the quiet become your foundation.)*
2. Stand & Command (2 mins)
   Stand tall. Hands on hips. Say:
   "I am the strategist. I own my energy. I create outcomes."

3. Physical Anchor (3 mins)
   Move your body to wake power.
   - 15 jumping jacks
   - OR splash face with cold water
   - OR 1 min fire breath (Kapalabhati)
4. Vision Lock (2 mins)
   Close your eyes and envision:
   - One thing you will finish today
   - One future you already own (visualize a future version of yourself or your life- as if it's already real)
5. Quick Strategy (1 min)
   Write down:
   - Today's one big goal
   - One emotion to lead with (power/positivity/ clarity etc.)
   - One thing you won't allow (comparison/ self- depreciation etc.)

2. Night Reset Protocol

You don't go to bed with war still inside you.

This ritual is not optional. It prevents carryover of static, shame, or scattered focus.

- Write 3 bullet points: What I built (action taken- what I created or achieved today) / What I burned (what I released or let go of) / What I claim (what I now choose to step into or declare as mine)
- 60 seconds: Breath + Stillness
- Final command: "I sleep in strength. I rise in command."

3. Sacred Workspace

Even if it's a corner. It must feel like a temple of mission.

- No clutter. No energy leaks.
- A talisman or symbol of your empire.
- Digital boundary: Only tabs/tools that serve the mission.

4. Weekly War Map

Every week begins with a sovereign strategy.

- **Power Goal** *(your main outcome)* – Example: Apply for two jobs, wake up at 7 a.m. daily, declutter your workspace, eat clean, or commit to regular workouts.
- **Three Impact Moves** *(aligned daily actions)* – Example: Update your CV, cut down on sugar for a week, stop scrolling after 10 p.m., or avoid caffeine after 2 p.m.
- **Guardrails** (What you refuse this week — distractions, guilt spirals, comparison, etc.)

Phase III. Tools of the Inner Ruler

1. Your Codex / Grimoire / Empire Book
   A physical or digital document where you write and record every decree, realization, ritual, and power law.
   This is not a journal. This is a manuscript of your mind.
2. The Hour of One
   At least once a week, devote an hour to complete solitude — no content, no input of any kind. Not a book, not a newspaper, not even the dull hum of television. Nothing but you and the vast empire of your own mind. What arrives in that silence will astonish you.

3. 3-Layered Financial Ritual:

You don't wait for money. You call it, move with it, and track it like a general.

- Money Magnetism Ritual (done weekly)- Refer to Zigrex Codex chapter 6
- Daily micro-wealth action (e.g., save 10- 100rs every day, send one follow-up to a client/prospect, track one overdue payment, and follow up- an old friend whom you had lent money to, perhaps)
- Weekly cash map: Incoming (what money is confirmed to come this week) / Stagnant (money that is stuck, pending, or forgotten) / Command Moves (what will I do this week to shift the situation)

Phase IV. The Mindset of Empire

- You are a builder, not a beggar. You no longer wait for validation, help, or luck. You architect.
- Emotion is energy. Direction is power. You don't get swept by moods. You channel them.
- Consistency is sacred. If it isn't sustainable, it's not sovereignty. Take slow, strong, strategic steps.
- You never speak weakness into ritual. No "I can't," "I'm trying," or "someday." Only use command language:

"I own it. I live it. I do. It is done."

Phase V. Framework for the Month of Empire

- Week 1: Foundation Building — Rituals, workspace, decrees (you set your environment and energetic tone. You create internal order before external results)
- Week 2: Energy Command — Food, sleep, movement, silence (energetic discipline- you are tuning your body temple to handle the weight of your empire. No empire is built by a zombie. Food fuels your brain. Movement is power. Sleep restores you with oxygen, flooding your body with repair and clarity. Silence conserves your energy, guarding it for what truly matters.
- Week 3: Power Outputs — Launches, content, conversions, actions (execute, lead, command- forward-moving actions that convert energy into results)
- Week 4: Audit & Ascend — What worked / What cracked / What now (this isn't self-pity or guilt journaling- this is empire analytics)

Phase VI. The Closing Vow: Sovereignty Over Sympathy

You are not waiting to be rescued.
You are not depending on anyone to see your worth.
You are not available for repeated derailment.

This Empire is not an act. It is your new default.
From today, you do not chase power. You systemize it.
You do not hope to rise. You make it inevitable.

Say it. Now.

> *"I rule my inner empire. I build, I command, I endure, I ascend."*

Here are a few examples of rituals and decrees

Rituals e.g.,: *Clearing the clutter, setting your workspace in order, rising/ resting at chosen hours—these rituals anchor your rhythm. Incense, stones, salts, or crystals can heighten the frequency of your space.*

Decrees e.g.,: *"This month, I do not chase, seek approval, or drain energy on ghosts."*

"I take command of my finances this week, and I track with precision where every penny flows."

When Syntax Snaps

Crayon elbow turbulence whispers midnight
Flannel spoons tap-dance on velvet regrets
Moisture calculators sing in whispering ketchup
Umbrella dignity turns sideways in marzipan
Cobwebs argue with sentimental doorknobs

Clockwise broccoli flirts with antique teaspoons
Panther jazz bleeds out of carbonated pillows
Feather lawsuits duel over salted oxygen
Satin remorse drinks a battery cocktail
Banana static hums in binary betrayal

Parrot-riddled shoelaces gum the choir's calculus
Ink-dripped chandeliers confess to thermos priests
Chalkboard lullabies thunder in sideways ballet
Napkin kingdoms dissolve in almond anarchy
Papercut empires swallow whispering antlers

Flim-flam flickers flip frilly flimsy flutes
Twiddle-tattle tickles tiny tinkling toads
Sizzle-snaps shimmer on slippery soap
Brickle-brackle blinks break brittle bricks
Flitter-fatter faster flutter flatter flops

Gweelop morzint flarbledoo kex
Plombyth rindle snaxor blitzzit
Zhoonk trapplest glirmb wock
Draxxlequint froom meggle-zik
Hhhhhlhhh... splunnnnnk... quurrrrz.
rrrRRRRRRRRRRRRRRrrrrrrrrrRRRRRRRrrrRRRrrrrrrr

SESSION X

POWER FINALE: THE ZIGREX DECLARATION

A Written and Spoken Declaration of Your New Self. No Turning Back

This is not a summary.
This is not a conclusion.
This is a final ignition.

The old you has been incinerated — in silence, in fire, in refusal.
This last session is the *lock*, the *seal*, the *spell*.
Once spoken, there is no going back.

You are no longer a seeker.
You are no longer fractured.
You are Zigrex — a name, a code, a command.

What This Declaration Is

- It is a vow to your own rebirth.
- It is the energy field you project into your choices, days, relationships, business, and body.

- It is the command code you activate when doubt or pullback tries to crawl back in.

You don't recite this.
You summon it.
You own it.
You bleed it.

The Zigrex Declaration

I am no longer available for smallness, silence, or submission.
I have buried the ghost of needing to be understood.
I no longer explain, beg, delay, or dilute.
I am not the version of me that cried in corners or pleaded with fate.
That version is gone. Burned. Buried. Banished.

I speak now as the architect of my destiny.
I command my thoughts. I command my energy.
I command my world into alignment.

I do not ask for a seat. I *build goddamn the throne.*
I do not seek love from the empty. I *radiate power* from fullness.
I do not chase money. I *summon it through clarity, fire, and precision.*

I am Zigrex.
Not a name — a frequency.
A code of returnless rise.
A force that no longer wavers, waits, or wounds.

My empire begins here.
My alignment is complete.
My word is law.
My power is permanent.
My evolution is non-negotiable-" **It is done."**

Instructions for Activation

- **Inscribe** — Let the declaration pass from your hand to the page, written in your own script, sealed with your full name and the word *Zigrex*. What is written is witnessed.
- **Proclaim** — Speak it aloud. Spine unbent, voice unwavering, energy unshaken. A titan does not whisper; a titan commands.
- **Anchor** — Forge a symbol for this vow — a mark, a sigil, an emblem, a piece of metal, a digital seal, a relic you choose. Place it where your eyes will fall upon it daily. It is not memory you are summoning, but frequency. The declaration must live in your field.

Place it where you *see it every day.*
It is no longer about memory. It is about frequency.
This declaration must enter your field and stay there.

Afterword: There is No Going Back

If you ever doubt again, you return to the declaration.
You read it aloud until your cells remember.

Because from this day,
you are not rebuilding. You are reigning.
Not hoping. Happening.
Not wounded. Weaponized.

Zigrex is now in motion.
So are you.

AUTHOR'S NOTE

The Journey of Zigrex: From Aviation to Awakening

At the close of 2022, I made one of the most defining decisions of my life: I walked away from a thriving career in business aviation. On paper, my trajectory had been enviable — I was excelling in my role, entrusted with responsibility, and had even pioneered the cabin safety training division as the company's very first safety manager. Yet beneath the surface, the environment had begun to corrode. New faces joined, and with them came deeper fissures of politics, pettiness, and hostility.

An incident with a newly inducted pilot crystallized this decline. I stood my ground, and in return, he refused to fly with me. In charter aviation, where crew numbers are minimal, such a refusal is not trivial — it makes you redundant, grounded, and erased. Management, rather than safeguarding the dignity of someone who had built systems for them without charging a penny, chose silence. They did not ask me to stay, did not consider what it would mean for me to leave. And so, I chose dignity over humiliation, even if it meant walking into uncertainty with no safety net.

The following years, 2023 and 2024, tested me beyond measure. Stripped of income, my savings began to erode, and though I tried relentlessly to re-enter aviation, every attempt dissolved into nothingness. Perhaps the universe was whispering a harsher truth — that the skies I once belonged to were no longer mine to claim. At the edge of despair, I understood that I could not merely wait for a door to open. I had to build one.

Thus was born **Zigrex**. What began as an ambitious loungewear brand soon revealed the realities of capital, infrastructure, and the indifference of financial institutions. Banks turned away. Investors showed no faith. I had no wealthy benefactors to fall back on, and even those closest to me were grappling with their own storms. The weight of survival rested squarely on my shoulders. And under that weight, my spirit began to fracture. Each day felt like a question I did not want to answer. Without purpose, life itself began to feel like an uninhabitable space.

But I am not one to surrender. When silence threatened to consume me, I turned to writing. Words became my salvation. I began shaping the **Zigrex Codex** — rituals and reflections distilled from my own search for meaning and resilience. Writing gave me breath where despair had taken it away. I blogged, I drafted, I created. Slowly, the work became my mirror, showing me a self I thought I had lost.

In time, I invested what little remained of my savings and heirlooms into publishing. And when *Zigrex Codex* was released, it was met with resonance. No, not in riches — but in recognition. In voices that said, *your words mattered.* That was wealth enough to begin again. Today, alongside the **Zigrex Power Coaching Series**, my work has expanded into helping others recalibrate their inner compass, as I once had to do for myself.

My journey spans over 13 years in both commercial and business aviation, where I held positions of trust — from cabin crew to in-flight manager, to director of cabin safety. I have trained, I have led, I have built, and I have endured. I have gained, lost, risen, and fallen. And yet, every collapse has been a raw material for reinvention.

This is my story: not of defeat, but of reclamation. Not of what was taken, but of what I chose to create. **Zigrex is not merely a brand. It is my declaration of sovereignty, resilience, and renewal.**

The Language Beyond Language

Throughout this book, you'll find stanzas of gibberish — fractured syllables, disjointed words, erratic rhythms, and nonsensical sounds. They follow many of my essays like ghosts trailing behind emotions. These aren't literary experiments. They are breakdowns. They are outbursts. They are what happens when the mind short-circuits and language — neat and polished — simply cannot keep up.

This gibberish is my *coping mechanism*. It's the scream under the whisper, the raw nerve exposed after thought. When I am anxious, over-stimulated, or emotionally cornered, I turn to this kind of expression. There's a strange relief in letting the mouth move faster than the mind, in letting sound spill without it making sense. It untangles something inside.

In a world that demands explanation, gibberish gives me permission to just *exist*. It holds the chaos without judgment. It echoes the absurdity of grief, the loops of obsession, the madness of waiting, loving, unraveling.

You don't have to make sense of it. In fact, I hope you resist the urge to.

And at the end of the day, what are we? Nothing more than glorified animals. The most dangerous of the tribe. Flesh and bones stitched together by hunger, desire, and decay. We build kingdoms, write scriptures, invent gods- yet strip it bare; you will not find gods- only carnivores of the spirit sharpening their teeth.